The King's Daughter

Reclaiming Your Royal Identity

By

Rolanda Gibson

Published by Rolanda Gibson Ministries

ISBN-13: 978-0-692-04853-5

Dedication

To My Lord and Savior, Jesus. Thank you for saving me and for creating me on purpose for purpose. Thank you for giving me the inspiration and the courage to write this book. Thank you for your guidance and work in my life. I love you!

To my parents Thomas and Rose Gibson. You are a true example of unconditional love. I am so thankful the Lord chose you to be my parents. The sacrifices you've made and continue to make will never be forgotten. I love you both!

Acknowledgements

Many thanks to Evangelist Barbara W. Green. Thank you for reading and editing my manuscript and for always pushing me to do more and challenging me to go further. You are loved and appreciated!

To Dr. Carolyn Hunt. I am grateful to God for allowing our paths to cross. Thank you for accepting and embracing me, and allowing me to learn from your wisdom. You are a blessing!

Foreword

Wow! Get ready to be blessed and refreshed in your love relationship with God! God is awesome! He is good! His desire is for each of us to know who we were created to be. He must have known the body of Christ needed an awesome and uncompromising message on *The King's Daughter: Reclaiming Your Royal Identity.*

Whether you have been walking in the blessings of God your whole life, recently accepted Jesus Christ as your Lord and Savior, or you're somewhere between the two, *The King's Daughter* will help reveal your mission in life and give you the strength to live your life based on your uniqueness and gifting's.

Minister Gibson's approach to this issue is not from a legalistic point of view, she has one motivation; to help women understand they are tailored made with a *Royal Identity!* Minister Gibson gives powerful insights on having a God-given vision and explains how being unique and original is a necessary part of God's purpose and plan for our lives. You will learn how you can nourish and activate your faith by reinvesting every portion of your life in God, drawing on the power of His Holy Spirit and His unique design of who you are.

You will find yourself being armed to silence the voice of condemnation that tries to bring up your past in an attempt to convince you that your Heavenly Father strongly disapproves of you and is determined to punish you for your shortcomings and mistakes.

In *The King's Daughter,* God wants to show us our true worth and value from His perspective as our Father. God wants you to know that you are valuable and precious and that He has placed kingdom treasures and gifts on the inside of you that are indescribable.

This book will cause you to see the awesome strength and beauty that God has given to every woman. It will stir up the royalty in your heart and inspire you to rise above the daily grind of life and serve God with a renewed passion. This book gives a thorough and balanced presentation on the importance of knowing your heritage as a King's Daughter. The chapter *I AM* contains positive affirmations and confessions that are a powerful tool to use daily to help shape your reality.

In every generation, God raises up voices that speak with boldness and clarity the freedom found only in Jesus. Minister Rolanda Gibson is one of those voices. I have hands on knowledge of Minister Gibson and her ministry and with confidence I can write a foreword to this book because I believe what Minister Gibson is saying is right on!

She is an anointed bold speaker, and an extraordinary writer. This book will inspire you to be the royalty you were created to be and to fulfill your God-purposed role in establishing God's kingdom on earth. Read on, and be blessed by this mighty woman of God with an anointed message!

Carolyn Hunt, Author of *The Total Woman,* and Pastor of Walk In The Word Church, Monroe, Louisiana

Introduction

"So God created man in His own image, in the image of God created He him; male and female created He them." (Genesis 1:27)

According to the FTC (Federal Trade Commission), identity theft is the fastest growing crime in America. It's a crime which allows someone who has the right tools and the right "know how" to access and steal everything that identifies who you are. It's a crime that allows a faceless criminal to assume your identity, ruin your credit, empty your bank accounts and temporilarly hinders your authority to use your own name. The interesting thing about identity theft is that most victims don't realize they're victims until they try to gain access to something they know they had, only to discover it's no longer there. Identity theft is an equal opportunity crime, affecting people of all races, all ages and all economic backgrounds.

This book however, is not about natural identity theft. This book is about spiritual identity theft. Spiritual Identity Theft is when the enemy tries to rob us of who we are and what we have in Christ. I believe this crime has gone undetected in the church for years because often times as children of God, we have a tendency to forget that we have two identities: a natural identity and a spiritual identity. Our natural identity is who we say we are or who others' believe we are based on external factors. Our spiritual identity is who we are in Christ. Our spiritual identity is who God says we are, based on our relationship with His Son.

II Corinthians 5:17 says *"therefore if any man be in Christ, he is a new creature; old things are passed away and behold all things are become new."* As new creatures in Christ, we have been liberated from sin and death; empowered to impact the world for Jesus; qualified to be seated in heavenly places and authorized to take dominion. Our most valuable possession and our most valuable treasure is who we are in Christ. It is this possession and treasure (who we are in Christ), along with the liberation, empowerment, qualification and authorization that comes along with it, that the enemy desires to steal from unsuspecting Christians.

The King's Daughter: Reclaiming Your Royal Identity is about understanding our spiritual identity, that is, who we are in Christ. It is about exposing satan's plan to steal our identity in Christ, in an attempt to render us powerless and ineffective as children of God; and it's about understanding the importance of affirming and re-affirming our identity in Christ. As you read the pages of this book, it is my prayer that the Holy Spirit will reveal to you who you really are in Christ and the magnitude of what that really means. We are not daughters of "a King;" we are daughters of THE KING!

Romans 8:17 says, *"we are heirs of God, and joint-heirs with Christ."* It is our status as heirs of God and joint-heirs with Christ, that gives us the right to have victory in every area of our lives. You are *The King's Daughter.* Act like it, walk like it, talk like it, and live like it!

Rolanda Gibson

Table of Contents

Tailor Made

"But ye are a chosen generation, a royal priesthood, an holy nation, a peculiar people; that ye should shew forth the praises of Him who hath called you out of darkness into His marvelous light." (I Peter 2:9)

Chapter 1

Tailor Made

"I will praise thee; for I am fearfully and wonderfully made: marvelous are thy works; and that my soul knoweth right well." (Psalm 139:14)

Every year, millions of snowflakes fall, but not one of them are the same. As individuals, we too are as uniquely different as snowflakes. Being unique and original is a necessary part of God's purpose and plan for all of our lives. When we were created by God, He intentionally created us to be distinctively different. We were not created as a mass produced assembly line product with no thought or care. No, God loves variety and He wants us to understand that everything about us, our looks, desires, temperaments, habits, personality traits, etc. are *intentionally* different.

For many of us however, today's society often plays a role in whether or not we embrace the unique individual God created us to be. Many times when we hear the words "peer pressure," we have a tendency to only think of children and adolescents; however, adults can be affected by peer pressure as well. Peer

Pressure is defined as the direct influence on a person by members of their peer group to act, think or behave a certain way in order to be accepted, liked and respected. Whether we realize it or not, our desire to be accepted, liked and respected still has a tendency to affect our decision making as adults. It is this peer pressure or external influence which causes many of us to deny our own originality and have a lack of appreciation for the unique individual God created us to be.

Psalm 139:14 says *"I will praise thee; for I am fearfully and wonderfully made.* When you consider what it means to be fearfully and wonderfully made, you will find that it can be both a burden and a blessing. It can be a burden because if we dare walk in our originality, we take the risk of being criticized, judged, misunderstood, and excluded. On the other hand, being fearfully and wonderfully made can be a blessing because if we trust God enough to walk in our originality, we'll experience the joy of Him using us to fulfill His specific purpose and plan for our lives. We were made on purpose, for purpose. Everything we need to successfully fulfill God's purpose for our lives is already in us. The challenge that hinders many of us is we often overlook our own uniqueness and originality and imitate others instead. Our mission in life is not to live someone else's life and vision but to live our own based on who God created us to be.

Rolanda Gibson

Why spend a lifetime putting unnecessary pressure on yourself trying to be like someone else? Enjoy being you! Since the creation of Adam and Eve, God has never created anyone to be exactly alike. He intentionally created us as a designer's original. So in the words of *Oscar Wilde: "Be yourself; everyone else is already taken."*

Something that is tailor made has been specifically designed for a particular person or purpose. When we consider the uniqueness of God's creation, we'll find that every creature has been tailor made to do certain things based on God's purpose for its' existence. Some animals were designed to run, while others were designed to hop, swim, burrow, or fly; and each animal has a particular role to play based on how it was uniquely created. The same is true for us. We each have a specific role, and specific assignments we were created to carry out. Some of us were created to preach and teach the Gospel. Others were created to sing, serve, encourage, or show compassion and mercy towards others just to name a few. Whatever your role or assignment, you were uniquely designed by God to successfully accomplish and carry it out.

There lies within each of us hidden seeds of greatness which will only be discovered and developed when we live as the unique individuals God created us to be. The only person we should ever compare ourselves to and strive to imitate is Jesus. It's a dangerous practice to imitate and compare ourselves to others because spiritually speaking, imitation and comparison eventually lead to stagnation and death. Unfortunately, many of us don't realize that when we imitate and compare ourselves to others, we fall into a trap that has been set by the enemy to abort God's plan for our lives. If you intend to be successful in your walk with the Lord and live your life to its' fullest, then you must have the courage to be different.

Never be ashamed or afraid to be who God created you to be. We were all *Tailor Made* by God on purpose for purpose. Boldly embrace your authentic self with grace and style. You are, indeed, *Tailor Made*.

Rolanda Gibson

"For ye are all children of God by faith in Christ Jesus."
(Galatians 3:26)

Chapter 2

The King's Daughter

"For I know the thoughts that I think toward you, saith the Lord, thoughts of peace, and not of evil, to give you an expected end." (Jeremiah 29:11)

As women, young ladies, and little girls, we're all uniquely different from one another. We are various ages, we come in all shapes and sizes, and we have a variety of strengths and weaknesses. But in the words of Maya Angelou, *"I note the obvious differences between each sort and type, but we are more alike, my friends, than we are unalike."*

For every woman, young lady or little girl who has accepted Jesus as Lord and Savior, this chapter is about the life changing way we are alike. We are all *The King's Daughter.* We are members of our Heavenly Father's royal family and our official title is Princess. When we hear the word princess, we have a tendency to think of it only in the natural sense, never really considering the spiritual aspect of being a princess. Naturally speaking, being a princess is about looking beautiful. It's about wearing tiaras, elegant dresses and fancy shoes; but spiritually speaking, being a princess is about fulfilling God's purpose and destiny for our lives.

As *The King's Daughter,* God wants to show us our true worth and value from His perspective as our Father. As I mentioned earlier, our royal title as Princess has nothing to do with being beautiful, wearing tiaras, elegant dresses and fancy shoes but being a Princess, being *The King's Daughter* is about purpose. Knowing our worth and value as daughters is essential if we're going to successfully fulfill God's purpose for our lives. As a Father, God wants us to know that we are valuable and precious and that He has placed treasures and gifts on the inside of us and has prepared wonderful things for our lives. Our Heavenly Father wants us to know that as His daughters, we are loved, cherished, valued, protected and will never be rejected or abandoned by Him.

Keeping that in mind, listed below are eight assurances we have from our Heavenly Father.

(1) We can approach God our Father with confidence without fear of being rejected (Hebrews 4:16).

(2) We will never be left alone or forsaken (Hebrews 13:5).

(3) Our needs will always be met (Philippians 4:19).

(4) We can bring our cares, worries, frustrations, and joys to Him freely and safely (I Peter 5:7).

(5) We are uniquely created (Psalm 139:14).

(6) Our Heavenly Father delights in giving us good things (Matthew 7:9-11).

(7) He has given us all the blessings of heaven (Ephesians 1:3).

(8) Nothing will separate us from His love (Romans 8:38-39).

As *The King's Daughter,* God has a special place in His heart for us all. We are so special to God, that the Bible tells us in *Isaiah 49:16* that *"God has written our names on the palms of His hand; and our walls are continually before Him."* Translation, as God's children, we are permanently in His hands, under His care, protection and provision. We can rest and take comfort in the fact that we have a Heavenly Father who loves us unconditionally, desires to have a father-daughter relationship with us, will never reject or abandon us and will always, ALWAYS keep His promises to us.

Attributes of our Heavenly Father

Trustworthy (Numbers 23:19)

Holy (Psalm 99:9)

Everlasting (Isaiah 40:28)

Keeper (Psalms 121:5)

Immutable (Malachi 3:6)

Near (Psalm 145:18)

Gracious (Jonah 4:2)

Strong Tower (Proverbs 18:10)

Deliverer (Psalm 18:2)

Anchor (Hebrews 6:18-19)

Undefiled (Hebrews 7:26)

Guide (Psalm 73:24)

Healer (Exodus 15:26)

Truth (John 14:6)

Eternal (Psalm 102:12)

Righteous (Psalm 145:17)

The Chatterbox

"For God sent not His Son into the world to condemn the world; but that the world through Him might be saved. He that believeth on Him is not condemned: but he that believeth not is condemned already, because he hath not believed in the name of the only begotten Son of God." (John 3:17-18)

Chapter 3

The Chatterbox

"There is therefore now no condemnation to them which are in Christ Jesus, who walk not after the flesh, but after the Spirit."
(Romans 8:1)

The Chatterbox. The Chatterbox? Yes, The Chatterbox. What is a Chatterbox? A chatterbox is someone who talks constantly. However, this chapter isn't about a person who talks constantly, this chapter is about a *voice* that talks constantly.

You know, the voice that talks to you all day everyday telling you you're "not good enough," you're "a failure," "you've messed up too many times for God to use you," "nothing will ever change in your life," and "God is so disappointed with you." The voice in your mind that greets you in the morning when you wake up, harasses you throughout the day and goes to bed with you at night. The voice that plays the same record over and over again, day in and day out and never shuts up. The Chatterbox, or in this chapter, the voice of condemnation. The word *condemnation* means to express strong disapproval of, or to pronounce judgment against. It means to sentence, or to declare to be unfit. The voice of condemnation is more than a voice, it's a spirit; and to be more specific, it's an accusing spirit. This spirit specializes in bringing up our past in an attempt to convince us that our Heavenly Father strongly disapproves of us and is determined to judge and punish us for our shortcomings and mistakes.

The voice of condemnation has paid us all a visit, and if we are honest, it still visits many of us today. So if we are going to silence this chatterbox once and for all, then there is something we need to understand about this accusing spirit; and that is this, it has absolutely nothing to do with our past. Yes, that's right, even though it constantly reminds us of our past, the voice of condemnation is not about where we've been but it's about where we are going. The enemy uses condemnation to build strongholds in our mind with the intent of wearing us down spiritually. If he can do this, he is one step closer to stopping us from accomplishing God's purpose for our lives.

Condemnation is a deceptive plan that has been designed by the enemy to constantly bring up and use our negative experiences to cause us to walk in guilt and shame. Condemnation thrives on reminding us of past failures, which ultimately leads to the Believer living an oppressed life: mentally, spiritually and emotionally.

But be of good cheer! Jesus Christ wants to set you free from the spirit of condemnation! BUT, we must do our part to defeat this spirit in our lives. There are three steps I want to share with you to help you overcome the spirit of condemnation.

The first step to overcoming is acknowledging and admitting the mistakes and bad decisions you have made (if you haven't done so already). Sometimes we give the enemy a legal right to attack us with the spirit of condemnation because we refuse to admit that we've made mistakes and bad decisions. Admitting our mistakes is not always easy but it's always necessary. Acknowledge it, admit it, and move on.

The second step to overcoming the spirit of condemnation is understanding the difference between condemnation and conviction. The Bible tells us in *Romans 8:1 "there is therefore now no condemnation to them which are in Christ Jesus, who walk not after the flesh, but after the Spirit."* It is important for us to understand that if we have accepted Jesus as our Lord and Savior, He will NEVER condemn us for our sins, mistakes and bad decisions, He will convict us. Let's take a closer look at the two words and what they are designed to do.

Condemnation	Conviction
Comes from the enemy	Comes from God
Designed to pass judgment or declare someone guilty with no hope of redemption	Designed to make someone aware of sin with the hope of them coming to Christ to receive redemption and restoration
Wants to destroy you	Wants to save you
Shows you the problem	Shows you the answer (Jesus)
Leads to a life of oppression	Leads to a life of Peace
Stops you from growing	Allows you to flourish
Causes spiritual, mental, and emotional death	Brings spiritual, mental, and emotional life

The spirit of condemnation is the exact opposite of the Spirit of God because it destroys and tears down, rather than encourages and builds up. The quicker you understand the difference between condemnation and conviction, the quicker you can be set free to move forward in accomplishing God's purpose for your life.

The third and final step to overcoming the spirit of condemnation is learning to recognize its' voice. I named this chapter *The Chatterbox* because the voice of condemnation will never be silenced unless you learn to recognize it and defeat it with the Word of God. *II Corinthians 10:4-5 says "for the weapons of our warfare are not carnal, but mighty through God to the pulling down of strongholds; casting down imaginations, and every high thing that exalteth itself against the knowledge of God, and bringing into captivity every thought to the obedience of Christ."*

As children of God we must learn to take control of the thoughts that bring the voice of condemnation. We must learn to cast down imaginations and bring into captivity every thought that does not reflect Christ or His nature. How can this be done? First, according to *Romans 12:1* we must diligently renew our minds on a daily basis with the Word of God and second, we must follow the instructions of the Apostle Paul in *Philippians 4:8, "whatsoever things are true, whatsoever things are honest, whatsoever things are just, whatsoever things are pure, whatsoever things are lovely, whatsoever things are of good report; if there be any virtue, and if there be any praise, think on these things."*

The Chatterbox, or the voice of condemnation desires that we walk in constant guilt and shame so we will never feel worthy of God's wonderful plan for our lives. Many of us are no longer growing in our walk and relationship with God because we have allowed the spirit of condemnation to rule in our lives. This causes us to focus on what has been, instead of focusing on what can be. Turn the tables on your past by silencing the voice of condemnation in your life once and for all. Remember, *"God knows the thoughts that He thinks toward you,* and they are *thoughts of peace, and not of evil, to give you an expected end."* *(Jeremiah 29:11).*

Rolanda Gibson

"The Spirit itself (Himself) beareth witness with our spirit, that we are the children of God; and if children, then heirs; heirs of God, and joint-heirs with Christ." (Romans 8:16-17a)

Chapter 4

Overcoming Identity Theft

"The thief cometh not, but for to steal, and to kill, and to destroy: I am come that they might have life, and that they might have it more abundantly." (John 10:10)

In spite of the many efforts designed to combat it, identity theft is still the fastest growing crime in America. According to a 2017 Identity Fraud Study released by Javelin Strategy and Research; in 2016, 15.4 million people or 1 in every 6 adults were victims of some form of identity theft. But as I mentioned in the introduction, this book isn't about overcoming natural identity theft, this book is about overcoming spiritual identity theft. As careful as we are about guarding our natural identity, far too often we are not as careful about guarding our *spiritual* identity.

Because of television commercials, radio announcements, news stories and advertisements that come in the mail, the alarm on natural identity theft has been sounded loud and clear. But as it relates to spiritual identity theft, as it relates to the millions of Christians whom satan has deceived, lied to, and convinced they are worthless and unredeemable, no alarm has been sounded. As a result, week in and week out, our churches are filled with Christians who are living defeated and unfulfilled lives. Why? Their spiritual identity, who they are in Christ, their purpose and reason for existence has been stolen by the enemy. In the natural realm, identities are stolen through credit cards, bank accounts, medical records and insurance policies; but in the spiritual realm, identities are stolen through condemnation, intimidation, insecurity, low self-esteem, guilt and shame.

Hosea 4:6 says *"my people are destroyed for lack of knowledge."* Spiritual Identity Theft is a concept that is unfamiliar to many in the Christian community. There is very little and in some instances no knowledge at all concerning it. As a result, I believe that spiritual identity theft has become the most destructive crime in the church today. At this point, you may be asking what is spiritual identity theft? Spiritual identity theft is when the enemy tries to rob us of who we are and what we have in Christ. It is when the enemy tries to manipulate our belief in who God created us to be. Spiritual identity theft occurs when we allow the enemy to constantly remind us of our past mistakes, sins, faults and failures; which causes us to feel unworthy and inadequate. In turn, we begin to doubt our value to God and doubt His ability to use us for His Glory.

II Corinthians 5:17 says *"therefore if any man be in Christ, he is a new creature; old things are passed away and behold all things are become new."* When we accept Jesus as our Lord and Savior, God comes to dwell or live on the inside of us. The moment this happens' we have the potential to be powerful beyond measure. The moment Christ comes to live on the inside of us, we become a threat to the powers of darkness. But because of the thief, too many sons and daughters of God are being denied the power and authority that is rightfully theirs.

As you continue to read this chapter, there are several things I want to establish beginning with the words of Jesus that are recorded in *John 10:10. "The thief cometh not, but for to steal, and to kill, and to destroy."* The first thing I want to establish is that in order to have a theft, there must first be a thief. A thief is a person who steals, especially secretly. The main objective of a thief is to take something that belongs to someone else with the intention of permanently depriving the owner of its' use. This is satan's modus operandi when it comes to stealing the spiritual identity of Christians. He works secretly through condemnation, intimidation, insecurity, low self-esteem, guilt and shame. His intent? To permanently deprive us as children of God of the power and authority God has given us, so he can stop us from impacting the world for Jesus.

Far too often, the thief is successful in stealing the spiritual identity of Christians because most Christians never knew who they were in Christ to begin with. As Christians, it is important for us to understand that the only advantage satan has over us is our ignorance. Just because we don't realize who we are and what we have in Christ doesn't mean it can't be stolen. Our ignorance or lack of knowledge of who we are and what we have just makes it easier to steal.

The second thing I want to establish is who we are in Christ. Once we have a clear understanding and a firm grasp on who we are in Christ, the chances of our spiritual identity being stolen is greatly diminished. So who are we in Christ? Let's take a look at the following scriptures to find out. Now you'll notice that each of the following scriptures have words missing and the reason for that is very simple, I want you to take an active role in discovering your identity in Christ. As you read each scripture, fill in the missing words to help you discover your identity in Christ.

1. And the _____ shall make thee the _____ and not the tail; and thou shalt be _____ _____, and thou shalt not be beneath (Deuteronomy 28:13).

2. *If the _____ therefore shall make you*
    _____, ye shall be _____
    _____ (John 8:36).

3. *There is therefore now _____*
    _____ to them which are in Christ Jesus, who
    walk not after the flesh, but _____
    _____ _____ (Romans 8:1).

4. *And if children, then _____;*
    _____ of _____, and
    _____-_____ with
    _____ (Romans 8:17).

5. *Nay, in all these things we are _____ than*
    _____ through _____ that loved us
    (Romans 8:37).

6. *Now then we are _____for*
    _____ (II Corinthians 5:20).

7. *For He hath made Him to be sin for us, who knew no sin; that we might be made the _____ of _____ in _____ (II Corinthians 5:21).*

8. *For we are _____ _____, _____ in _____ _____ unto good works, which God hath before ordained that we should walk in them (Ephesians 2:10).*

9. *And ye are _____ in _____ which is the head of all principality and power (Colossians 2:10).*

10. *But ye are a _____ _____, a _____, an _____ _____, a _____ _____; that ye should shew forth the praises of Him who hath _____ _____ out of _____ into His _____ _____ (I Peter 2:9).*

When God sees us, He sees greatness, beauty, potential and promise. When God sees us, He sees us walking in victory in every area of our lives. In order to successfully stop the enemy from stealing our spiritual identity, we must see ourselves the way God sees us. WHOLE, FORGIVEN, REDEEMED, VALUABLE, and PRECIOUS.

The third and final point I want to establish is understanding the power of our words. Not only is it important to see ourselves the way God sees us, but it's also important to remind ourselves of who we are in Christ. People often say it's not good to talk to yourself, and depending on what you're saying to yourself about yourself, they may be right. But I've come to learn that in order to stop our spiritual identity from being stolen, we must constantly remind ourselves of who we are in Christ. One of the most effective ways of doing so is by using our words to encourage ourselves. The next chapter, *I AM,* is designed to help you use the power of your words to encourage yourself and affirm your identity in Christ.

Never allow the enemy to cause you to doubt your worth and value to God or to yourself. Always let your identity rest in the truth of God's Word. You are *The King's Daughter!*

Rolanda Gibson

"Pleasant words are as an honeycomb, sweet to the soul, and health to the bones." (Proverbs 16:24)

Chapter 5

I AM

"Let the words of my mouth, and the meditation of my heart, be acceptable in thy sight, O Lord, my strength, and my redeemer." (Psalm 19:14)

The ability to use words is a unique and powerful gift from God. From Genesis to Revelation, the Bible is filled with scriptures concerning the power of our words. When used to accomplish good, words can restore, revitalize, refresh, and encourage. On the other hand, when used to cause harm, words can demean, devalue, devastate, and tear down.

Words are designed to convey thoughts and ideas and they are powerful enough to manifest and bring into existence everything we say. *I AM* are two of the most powerful words in our vocabulary because what we say after them will shape our reality. Whether you realize it or not, we frame our world with our words. The Bible says in *Proverbs 18:21* that *"death and life are in the power of the tongue: and they that love it shall eat the fruit thereof."* Every day we speak a countless number of words and many times, without even realizing it, we are framing our world with words of death and failure instead of life and success. All through the day the words we speak are at work in our lives, and whatever we speak will eventually find us.

Consider your words. Are they filled with love or hate, compliments or complaining, blessings or bitterness, victory or defeat? Do they inspire or destroy? Do they activate faith or doubt? If your present reality isn't what you want it to be, it could be a result of the words you are speaking. Steve Furtick said, *"if you want to change the direction of your life, change the declaration of your lips."*

This chapter is designed to help you change the declaration of your lips from death and failure to life and success. Let's take a closer look at the words *I AM* so we can gain a better understanding of why they are so powerful. The word *I* is a singular pronoun that represents the person speaking. The word *AM* is used to describe the identity and qualities of a person or thing. When we say *I AM,* we are actually saying we identify with and possess the qualities of whatever follows those two words whether they are positive or negative.

For example, if you say *I AM* successful, what you are really saying is that you identify with and possess the qualities of a person who is productive and successful. On the other hand, if you say *I AM* a failure, you're saying that you identify with and possess the qualities of a person who is unproductive and never succeeds. *I AM* is a definitive statement of who we are that we proclaim to ourselves and to others.

Let's go deeper. In the Gospel of John, on seven separate occasions, Jesus used the phrase *I AM*. Each time Jesus used that phrase, He made specific revelations about His identity and nature.

The Seven I AMs of Jesus

1. I AM the Bread of Life: The Sustainer (John 6: 35, 41, 48 & 51).

Jesus fed those who were physically hungry, but His greatest concern was to feed those who were spiritually hungry. Jesus is the only bread that can feed, nourish and satisfy man's spiritual hunger.

2. I AM the Light of the world: The Illuminator (John 8:12; 9:5).

As the Light of the world, Jesus offers a choice between the darkness of sin and the light of life in His presence.

3. I AM the Door of the Sheep: The Mediator (John 10: 7, 9).

Jesus is the only way, the only true path that leads to salvation, God's presence and God's acceptance.

4. I AM the Good Shepherd: The Caretaker (John 10: 11, 14).

Jesus gave and sacrificed His life for the sheep.

5. I AM the Resurrection and the Life: The Life Giver (John 11:25).

Jesus is the very essence, power and energy of life; therefore, He can give, sustain, restore and resurrect life as He wills. He is the Source of ALL life.

6. I AM the Way, the Truth, and the Life: The Leader (John 14:6).

The only way to God is through Christ Himself.

7. I AM the True Vine: The Success Maker (John 15: 1, 5).

When we accept Jesus (the True Vine) as Lord and Savior, He gives us (the Branches) the Holy Spirit which produces fruit in our lives. Jesus (the True Vine) sustains and gives life to the Branches.

I AM

The I AMs of Jesus reveal to us the fullness of His character. He had no doubt about who He was or what He was, and the words He spoke about Himself manifested themselves in His everyday life. The same applies to us. If we want to see the power of God manifest in our lives, we must pay attention to the words we speak.

The following pages contain 365 affirmations and positive confessions. Yes, one for every day of the year. You can write them on index cards, type or write them on strips of paper and place them in a jar or read one a day from the book. Whichever method you choose, I challenge you for the next year to quote and mediate on one affirmation/positive confession a day and allow them to rest in your spirit. As you say and mediate on them, they may not be your present reality, but as you continue to speak them, they will become your reality.

Daily Affirmations/Positive Confessions

1. Nothing will separate me from God's love.

2. The Lord will do great and mighty things through my life.

3. I will succeed at being myself.

4. I will bless the Lord at all times.

5. I refuse to be a prisoner of my past.

6. I am complete in Christ.

7. I am divinely protected.

8. The joy of the Lord is my strength.

9. I am valuable and precious to God.

10. I am a designer's original.

11. My life matters to God.

12. I am beautiful inside and out.

13. I will walk by faith and not by sight.

14. I am the head and not the tail.

15. The Lord has a good and perfect plan for my life.

16. I will become everything God created me to be.

17. I will soar like an eagle.

18. I will never give up.

19. I am intelligent.

20. I am an overcomer.

21. My strength is renewed day by day.

22. I am chosen by God.

23. I am good enough.

24. I am accepted and loved by God.

25. I am approved by God.

26. I am special, unique, gifted, loveable, valuable, and good enough just the way I am.

27. I will embrace and use the gifts God has given me.

28. The blessings of the Lord are running me down and taking me over.

29. I will trust God for the impossible.

30. I am beautiful.

31. I have unlimited potential.

32. I am a new creature in Christ.

33. My past does not have dominion over me.

34. I love and accept myself unconditionally.

35. I am free in Christ.

36. I am royalty.

37. With God all things are possible.

38. My best days are ahead of me.

39. God has great things in store for me.

40. The Lord is my light and salvation.

41. I am extraordinary.

42. I am a unique gift to the world.

43. I will trust in the Lord with all my heart.

44. My possibilities are endless.

45. I will fulfill God's purpose and destiny for my life.

46. I am brilliant, gorgeous, self-confident and fabulous.

47. I am a woman of faith.

48. I was born to manifest greatness.

49. Abundant blessings are coming my way.

50. God has placed seeds of greatness in me.

51. I am God's masterpiece.

52. I am more than a conqueror.

53. I am proud of myself.

54. I am the apple of God's eye.

55. God is my refuge and strength.

56. I am handpicked by God.

57. God is fighting my battles.

58. The Lord loves and accepts me unconditionally.

59. The Lord will give me beauty for ashes.

60. I am a blessing.

61. I am fearfully and wonderfully made.

62. I will live a blessed and prosperous life.

63. God's Grace is sufficient for me.

64. I appreciate myself.

65. I am a winner.

66. I am anointed.

67. I will celebrate myself.

68. Goodness and Mercy will follow me all the days of my life.

69. I am God's treasure.

70. Greater is He that is in me than he that is in the world.

71. I am strong in the Lord and in the power of His might.

72. I put a smile on God's face.

73. God loves me with an everlasting love.

74. I will never give up on God.

75. I am an Ambassador for Christ.

76. I am surrounded by God's favor.

77. My life has worth and value.

78. I have victory in every area of my life.

79. I am a wonderful person.

80. I expect great things from myself.

81. There are no limits to what I can achieve.

82. I am awesome.

83. The favor of God is on my life.

84. I am gifted and talented.

85. My future is bright.

86. I am worth loving.

87. God will never leave me nor forsake me.

88. I can do all things through Christ who strengthens me.

89. I am triumphant in Christ Jesus.

90. I am somebody because of Christ.

91. The Lord is my rock and my fortress.

92. I am made in God's image and after His likeness.

93. I am a wonderful expression of God's love.

94. I believe in myself and my abilities.

95. I am the lender and not the borrower.

96. Everything I touch will prosper and succeed.

97. I will not criticize or reject myself.

98. No weapon that is formed against me will prosper.

99. What's ahead of me is greater than what's behind me.

100. I have favor with God and man.

101. I will not grow weary in well doing.

102. I will cast all of my cares on Jesus.

103. I am anxious for nothing.

104. This is the day the Lord has made, I will rejoice and be glad in it.

105. I am blessed with the wisdom of God.

106. My enemies will not rejoice over me.

107. I will speak faith filled words.

108. I am the righteousness of God.

109. I will rejoice in the Lord.

110. I am anchored in Christ.

111. I am excited about my future.

112. I will use my words to edify, comfort and encourage others.

113. My life is a reflection of God's goodness.

114. The Lord has given His angels charge over me.

115. I am increasing in the knowledge of God.

116. I will hold fast to the profession of my faith.

117. The Lord rejoices over me with gladness and singing.

118. The Lord crowns me with loving kindness and tender mercies.

119. I am sealed with the Holy Spirit.

120. The Lord shall perfect everything that concerns me.

121. I will exercise faith and patience.

122. My latter days will be greater than my former days.

123. I am not afraid or dismayed because the Lord is always with me.

124. I respect and value myself.

125. The Lord will bless the works of my hands.

126. I have peace in my mind and joy in my heart.

127. I will live a long and satisfied life.

128. The Lord will do exceeding, abundantly above all that I ask or think, according to the power that works in me.

129. I possess and exhibit all the fruit of the Spirit.

130. I am healed by the stripes of Jesus.

131. I have the mind of Christ.

132. The Peace of God reigns in my life.

133. My God shall supply all of my needs according to His riches in glory by Christ Jesus.

134. My life overflows with the joy of the Lord.

135. I am well able to accomplish my dreams.

136. God has not given me the spirit of fear; but of power, and of love, and of a sound mind.

137. I will prosper and be in health even as my soul prospers.

138. I shall live and not die and declare the works of the Lord.

139. My gift will make room for me and bring me before great men.

140. The promises of God are manifesting in my life.

141. In Christ I live, move and have my being.

142. The Lord is my Keeper.

143. I will mediate on God's Word day and night.

144. The Lord shall preserve me from all evil.

145. I am above only and not beneath.

146. I am blessed in the city and blessed in the field.

147. No evil shall befall me and no plague shall come near my dwelling.

148. I am blessed going out and blessed coming in.

149. The Lord shall preserve my soul.

150. The Lord will not suffer my foot to be moved.

151. I will delight myself in the Lord.

152. The Lord is working all things together for my good.

153. The mercy of the Lord will hold me up.

154. I will keep my eyes on Jesus.

155. The Lord shall preserve my going out and my coming in.

156. I am blessed beyond measure.

157. The Lord is mindful of me.

158. The Lord will reward my faithfulness in due season.

159. I will declare the goodness of the Lord.

160. The Lord is on my side.

161. The Lord is my guide and provider.

162. The Lord knows my name.

163. I am a survivor.

164. The Lord will give me the desires of my heart.

165. I will not allow people or circumstances to steal my joy.

166. I am steadfast, unmovable, always abounding in the work of the Lord.

167. I am a doer, not just a hearer of the Word.

168. God causes all grace to abound toward me.

169. I will wait on the Lord and trust His timing.

170. I am adored by God.

171. The angel of the Lord encamps around me and delivers me.

172. I am who God says I am.

173. I am transformed daily by the renewing of my mind.

174. I will run and not grow weary, I will walk and not faint.

175. I am safe in the arms of Jesus.

176. I am blessed with the highest measure of God's favor.

177. The Lord will show Himself strong and mighty on my behalf.

178. I will finish my course.

179. I am dynamic.

180. I am celebrated with joy in heaven and on earth.

181. The Lord is the strength of my life.

182. I am blessed with the fullest portion of God's grace.

183. The Lord will make my enemies my footstool.

184. I will not live in fear.

185. I am forgiven.

186. I am cherished by God.

187. I am a woman of vision.

188. The Lord delights in me.

189. I am redeemed from the curse of the law.

190. The Lord is my strong tower and deliverer.

191. The Lord will renew, revive, and restore every area of my life.

192. The Lord will open doors for me that no man can close.

193. Fear does not have dominion over me.

194. I am a woman after God's own heart.

195. I am growing in grace.

196. I am overwhelmed by God's love.

197. I am a woman of purpose.

198. I am a child of the Most High God.

199. I am outstanding.

200. I am blessed with the deepest measure of God's love.

201. I am seated in heavenly places.

202. I will lay aside every weight and sin that so easily besets me.

203. God's Word is a lamp unto my feet and a light unto my path.

204. The Lord is my Jehovah-Chatsahi (Strength).

205. It's my winning season.

206. The Lord is my Jehovah-Maozi (Fortress).

207. I refuse to be intimidated by the enemy.

208. I am free from condemnation.

209. I shall lack no good thing.

210. The Lord is my strength and shield.

211. I am a chosen generation.

212. I am an imitator of Christ.

213. The Lord is my strength and song.

214. I have a thankful heart.

215. The Lord is my Jehovah-Jireh (Provider).

216. I am authorized to take dominion.

217. I am secure in who God created me to be.

218. I am free from low self-esteem.

219. I will praise the Lord for His excellent greatness.

220. I am incredible.

221. I am joint heirs with Christ Jesus.

222. The Lord is my Jehovah-Ezer (Help).

223. The Lord is my Jehovah-Magen (Shield).

224. I have confidence in myself.

225. I am empowered by God.

226. My God is faithful.

227. My steps are ordered by the Lord.

228. It is well with my soul.

229. I am unstoppable.

230. I am strong and courageous.

231. The Lord is my Jehovah-Nacham (Comforter).

232. I will not be afraid for the terror by night; nor for the arrow that flieth by day.

233. I have a cheerful and positive attitude.

234. I am resilient.

235. I am spectacular.

236. The Lord is my glory and the lifter of my head.

237. The Lord has crowned me with glory and honor.

238. I am great in the sight of God.

239. The Lord is my Jehovah-Misqabbi (High Tower).

240. The Lord is my Jehovah-Go'el (Redeemer).

241. I am remarkable.

242. The Lord will turn my sorrow into joy.

243. I will rest in the Lord and wait patiently for Him.

244. I am an heir of God.

245. I am victorious.

246. I was created on purpose for purpose.

247. I am clothed with strength and honor.

248. I am the King's Daughter.

249. I am capable of accomplishing great things.

250. I am worthwhile and valid.

251. I will stand on the promises of God.

252. I am thankful for what I have.

253. God's love for me has no limits.

254. The Lord has great things in store for me.

255. This is my season for breakthrough.

256. The Lord is my Jehovah-'Ori (Light).

257. The Lord is my Jehovah-Tiqvah (Hope).

258. I am tailor made.

259. The Lord is my portion.

260. I will give thanks unto the Lord for He is good.

261. I am a virtuous woman.

262. I am free from guilt and shame.

263. I will bless the name of the Lord forever.

264. The greatness of God is unsearchable.

265. The Lord is my Jehovah-Rapha (Healer).

266. I will praise the Lord with my whole heart.

267. I will sing unto the Lord as long as I live.

268. I will serve the Lord with gladness.

269. My value is far above rubies.

270. I am justified by faith.

271. I am God's handiwork; therefore, I will not compare myself to others.

272. I feel great about myself.

273. The Lord is my Jehovah-Manah (Portion).

274. I forgive myself.

275. Jesus is a friend who sticks closer than a brother.

276. I appreciate my blessings.

277. I will live life to its' fullest.

278. From the rising of the sun unto the going down of the same, I will praise the name of the Lord.

279. The Lord is my Jehovah-Kabodhi (Glory).

280. I am delivered from the powers of darkness.

281. God has a great investment in me.

282. I will walk in love.

283. Jesus is the author and finisher of my faith.

284. I walk in dominion and authority.

285. I am equipped with the full armor of God.

286. I am the light of the world.

287. I am saved by grace through faith.

288. The Lord is my Jehovah-Uzam (Strength in trouble).

289. God will use me for His Glory.

290. I am a mountain mover.

291. I am an instrument of righteousness.

292. I am prosperous.

293. I am the salt of the earth.

294. I am rooted in Christ.

295. I walk in the wisdom of God.

296. I am a friend of God.

297. The Lord is my Jehovah-Machsi (Refuge).

298. Nothing will separate me from God's love.

299. I am sanctified.

300. I am the temple of the Holy Spirit.

301. The Lord holds me in the palm of His hands.

302. I am in the world but not of the world.

303. God will turn my burdens into blessings.

304. I am blessed with all spiritual blessings.

305. My faith in God grows day by day.

306. The Lord will honor His Word in my life.

307. I will let my light shine before men.

308. I will believe the report of the Lord.

309. I am like a tree planted by the rivers of water.

310. I am fully committed to serving the Lord.

311. I am a reflection of God's beauty.

312. I am a jewel.

313. I am God's elect.

314. I am spiritually whole.

315. I am a woman of integrity.

316. Patience will have its perfect work in my life.

317. I am redeemed by the blood of Jesus.

318. The Lord will give me the garment of praise for the spirit of heaviness.

319. I am fruitful in every good work.

320. I am emotionally whole.

321. The Lord is my Jehovah Mephalti (Deliverer).

322. The Lord will turn my mourning into dancing.

323. I am a world changer.

324. God watches over His Word to perform it in my life.

325. I am a partaker of God's divine nature.

326. Greater is coming in every area of my life.

327. I see myself the way God sees me.

328. I am physically whole.

329. The Lord is my hiding place and my shield.

330. God's love for me is indescribable.

331. I am strong and mature in my faith.

332. My youth is renewed like the eagles.

333. The Lord is my Jehovah-Cheleq (Inheritance).

334. I am crucified with Christ.

335. My self-esteem is healthy.

336. I am not an accident or mistake. My life is ordained by God.

337. I see the best in myself.

338. The Lord is my Jehovah-M'Kaddesh (Sanctifier).

339. I am free from self-doubt.

340. I am filled with the Holy Spirit.

341. I will represent God with excellence.

342. I am set apart for purpose.

343. The Lord is my Jehovah-Nissi (Banner).

344. I am what I am by the grace of God.

345. God's Word will not return to me void.

346. I am mentally whole.

347. God will be glorified in my life.

348. I am creative.

349. Jesus is the center of my joy.

350. My God is bigger than my problems.

351. I am an inspiration to others.

352. I am worry free and stress free.

353. The Lord is my Jehovah-Ganan (Defense).

354. I am an achiever.

355. I will rest in God's faithfulness.

356. God sees the best in me.

357. I am always on God's mind.

358. The Lord is always with me.

359. The Lord is my Jehovah-Sel'i (Rock).

360. The Lord is my Jehovah-Shalom (Peace).

361. I am a Princess.

362. I am second to none.

363. God will use me to bless the nations.

364. I am priceless.

365. I am a phenomenal woman!

As *The King's Daughter*, we must come to a place in life where we learn to consider the impact of our words. *Romans 4:17* says to *"call those things that be not as though they were."* This simply means we shouldn't talk about the way things are but the way we want them to be. Do you really want to change your circumstances and the direction of your life for the better? If so, begin by disciplining yourself to speak in such a way that your words create life and produce positive results. Your words have power. Change your words and you will change your world.

About the Author

Minister Rolanda Gibson has an unwavering commitment to the Lord Jesus Christ, the integrity of His Holy Word, and a love for His people! Minister Gibson, a native of Baton Rouge, Louisiana is founder and CEO of Rolanda Gibson Ministries and DIAMONDS LEADERSHIP ACADEMY (DLA) which is a non-profit organization for young ladies in grades 6th-12th.

Answering her call to ministry at the age of 17, Minister Gibson has over 20 years of ministry experience. Her ministry experience includes service as an Associate Pastor, Youth Pastor, Adult Bible Study Teacher, Adult Sunday School Teacher and serving with the Nursing Home Ministry. Minister Gibson has been privileged to minister at numerous youth and adult workshops and conferences. The Lord has also graced her to author three books: *Now I Know, The King's Daughter and FAVOR: God's Exception To The Rule.*

Minister Gibson boldly declares the Word of God with uncompromised accuracy, clarity, power and authority. She is an anointed teacher and preacher who rightly divides the Word of God and is adamant about using God's Word to educate, equip, empower and impact the lives of others to live their best life now!

Her desire and call to teach and preach has provided her with many opportunities to share the Gospel of Jesus Christ with people of all ages. Minister Gibson believes *"the Spirit of the Lord is upon her, because He has anointed her to preach the Gospel to the poor; He has sent her to heal the broken-hearted, to preach deliverance to the captives, and recovering of sight to the blind, to set at liberty them that are bruised, to preach the acceptable year of the Lord" (Luke 4:18-19).*

To Contact the Author

Email: rgibsonministries@gmail.com or call (225) 372-8571.

www.ingramcontent.com/pod-product-compliance
Lightning Source LLC
Chambersburg PA
CBHW071949100426
42736CB00042B/2600